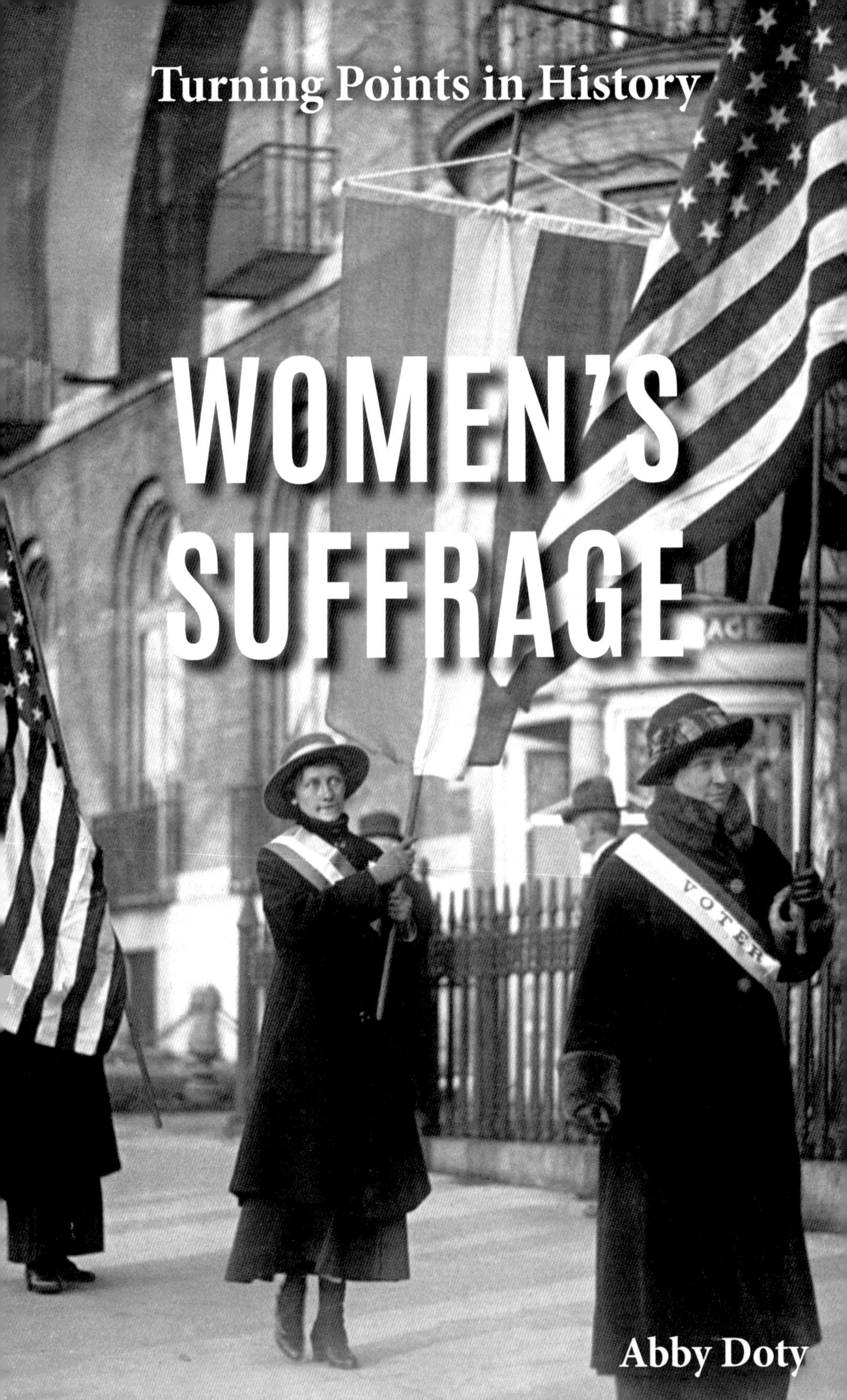
Turning Points in History
WOMEN'S SUFFRAGE
VOTER
Abby Doty

WWW.APEXEDITIONS.COM



Apex is distributed by North Star Editions:
sales@northstareditions.com | 888-417-0195

Produced for Apex by Red Line Editorial.

Photographs ©: Library of Congress, cover, 1, 10–11, 12–13, 16–17, 24–25, 26–27, 28–29, 44–45, 46–47; National Portrait Gallery/Smithsonian Institution, 4–5; Emanuel Tanjala/Alamy, 6–7; Harris & Ewing/Library of Congress, 8–9, 32–33, 34–35, 58; Victoria Stauffenberg/National Park Service, 14–15; Frances Benjamin Johnston/Library of Congress, 19; iStockphoto, 20–21; Bettmann/Getty Images, 22–23, 42–43; F. E. Redmond/Library of Congress, 30–31; National Archives, 36–37; Harris & Ewing/National Archives, 38–39; Chicago History Museum/Archive Photos/Getty Images, 41; Carl Deeg/Library of Congress, 48–49; Underwood Archives/Archive Photos/Getty Images, 50–51; Hartsook/Library of Congress/Corbis/VCG/Bettmann/Getty Images, 52–53; Warren K. Leffler/Library of Congress, 54–55; Shutterstock Images, 56–57

**Library of Congress Control Number: 2024943625**

**ISBN**
979-8-89250-467-6 (hardcover)
979-8-89250-483-6 (paperback)
979-8-89250-513-0 (ebook pdf)
979-8-89250-499-7 (hosted ebook)

Printed in the United States of America
Mankato, MN
012025

## NOTE TO PARENTS AND EDUCATORS

Apex books are designed to build literacy skills in striving readers. Exciting, high-interest content attracts and holds readers' attention. The text is carefully leveled to allow students to achieve success quickly.

# TABLE OF CONTENTS

Chapter 1

# GETTING THE VOTE

Activists marched through the streets of Nashville, Tennessee. They waved yellow banners. They also wore yellow roses on their shirts. The activists called for women's suffrage. Other people marched, too. They wore red roses. They opposed women's right to vote.

Activist Carrie Chapman Catt led the effort for women's voting rights in Tennessee.

On August 18, 1920, Tennessee lawmakers gathered. They voted on an amendment. It would give women voting rights. Many lawmakers voted against it. But many supported it. The vote ended in a tie. Lawmaker Harry T. Burn wore a red rose. But he changed his vote. Burn supported the amendment. He broke the tie.

## THE 36TH STATE

**Tennessee helped pass the Nineteenth Amendment to the US Constitution. The amendment gave women the right to vote. At least 36 states had to make the change. Tennessee was the 36th state to support it.**

Lawmaker Harry T. Burn (right) got a letter from his mother (left). She persuaded him to vote for women's voting rights.

Suffragists all over the country celebrated. In Washington, DC, women sat around activist Alice Paul. She stitched a 36th star onto a banner. Paul walked to an open window. She unrolled the long banner. It hung above a group of activists. They cheered around it. Women had won the right to vote.

Alice Paul unrolls the banner with 36 stars to celebrate the victory for women's voting rights.

Chapter 2

# EARLY WORK

The United States became a country in 1776. For many years, women had few rights. Most women couldn't own land. They couldn't vote. They couldn't run for office. Husbands controlled their wives' money and land.

Lucretia Mott was born in 1793. She went on to become a key leader in the struggle for women's rights.

Activist Sojourner Truth often linked rights for Black people with rights for women. She believed all people deserved equal treatment.

Women also faced strict gender roles. For example, many women were expected to stay at home. They were expected to be wives and mothers. In the early 1800s, some women began pushing back. They formed groups that called for change. Many teamed up with antislavery groups. Both struggles wanted equal rights.

## ANTISLAVERY LEADERS

**Sojourner Truth called for the end of slavery. She also fought for women's rights. Activist Frederick Douglass worked for the same causes. Both Truth and Douglass gave many powerful speeches.**

In July 1848, the Seneca Falls Convention took place in New York. Elizabeth Cady Stanton and Lucretia Mott set up this meeting. People there agreed that women should have equal rights. They created a list of 12 demands. One called for women to have the right to vote.

## STANTON AND MOTT

Elizabeth Cady Stanton and Lucretia Mott met in 1840. They went to an antislavery event. But they couldn't take part because they were women. The two talked about how unfair that was. This meeting led to the 1848 event in Seneca Falls, New York.

People can visit the building where the Seneca Falls Convention took place.

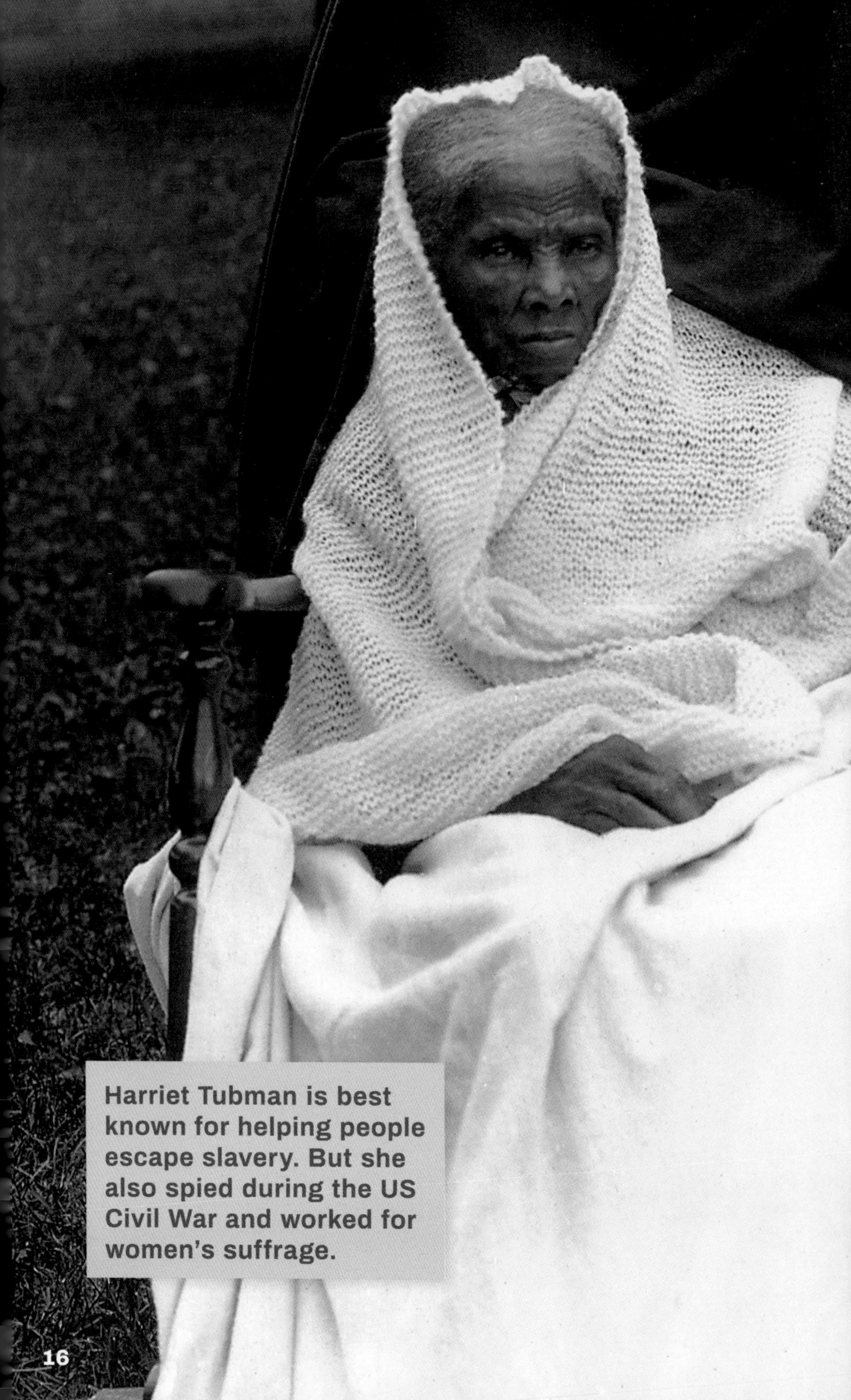

Harriet Tubman is best known for helping people escape slavery. But she also spied during the US Civil War and worked for women's suffrage.

The fight for voting rights slowed during the US Civil War (1861–1865). Instead, women focused on the war effort. Some helped as nurses. Some activists created the Women's Loyal National League. Stanton led this group. So did activist Susan B. Anthony. The group called for the end of slavery. It supported citizenship for freed Black people.

## Story Spotlight

# SUSAN B. ANTHONY

Susan B. Anthony supported many ideas. She worked to end slavery. She called for equal pay for women. She also fought for women's right to vote.

In 1851, Anthony started working with Elizabeth Cady Stanton. They traveled the country together. Anthony gave many speeches. She created petitions. In 1892, she became the president of a woman's suffrage group.

**Susan B. Anthony spent more than 50 years fighting for women's suffrage.**

Anthony died in 1906. That was 14 years before women got the right to vote. But her efforts were key to the movement.

By 2025, there had been 27 amendments to the US Constitution.

Chapter 3

# SPLIT GROUPS

After the Civil War was over, new amendments passed. The Fourteenth Amendment gave rights to citizens. Many people had wanted "citizens" to include women. But it included only men. The Fifteenth Amendment came next. It allowed Black men to vote.

In 1869, activists split into different groups. Elizabeth Cady Stanton and Susan B. Anthony formed one group. It was the National Woman Suffrage Association (NWSA). The NWSA fought for countrywide change. Members pushed for many rights. They cared about voting, divorce, and education.

## ONE SIDE

The NWSA opposed the Fifteenth Amendment. Some members did not want any change that didn't include women. Others used racist reasons. They said white women were smarter than Black people and deserved the vote more.

Susan B. Anthony (left) and Elizabeth Cady Stanton (right) both opposed the Fourteenth and Fifteenth Amendments.

Lucy Stone's American Woman Suffrage Association focused only on voting rights.

Other activists created a second group. It was the American Woman Suffrage Association (AWSA). Lucy Stone led this organization. The AWSA created change at the state and local levels. Members spoke with Congress. They sent in petitions. They started a newspaper about voting.

## THE OTHER SIDE

The AWSA supported the Fifteenth Amendment. The group knew lawmakers didn't support women's voting rights. Adding women to the amendment was a risk. It could have killed the amendment. So, the AWSA waited until it passed. They pushed for women's voting rights later.

Newspapers helped spread ideas about women's rights throughout the United States.

In 1890, the NWSA and AWSA joined together. They became the National American Woman Suffrage Association (NAWSA). This large movement was made up of smaller groups around the country. The groups hosted events. They spread their messages in newspapers.

## AROUND THE WORLD

NAWSA held a conference in 1902. It included multiple countries. Suffragists from all over the world came together. They spoke about their experiences as women. They formed a group. It fought for voting rights around the globe. Many countries joined.

Mary Church Terrell was the first leader of the National Association of Colored Women.

Many suffrage groups did not let women of color join. So in 1896, Black activists created their own group. It was the National Association of Colored Women (NACW). It focused on rights for women and Black Americans. It gave Black women their own space.

Chapter 4

# PROTESTS

Women used many arguments to gain support. Some activists pointed to the Fourteenth Amendment. One part said that anyone born in the United States was a citizen. So, American women should be citizens. Others said women were just as deserving as men. They were as smart as men. They followed laws like men.

Activists often spread their arguments using small pieces of paper called leaflets.

VOTES
FOR
WOMEN
BROADSIDE

Many people opposed women's voting rights. Some of these people were women. They believed in traditional roles. They thought women didn't belong in politics. Others thought politics would change family life. They believed politics led to bad behavior. And they felt their power in the family came from good character. Entering politics might cost women their character and that power. Some women argued the trade was not worth it.

The National Association Opposed to Woman Suffrage was one of the leading groups against voting rights for women.

An activist speaks to a US senator about women's suffrage in 1918.

Activists fought hard for voting rights. They held yearly events. They spread flyers and information. They spoke out against injustices. Some women went to the US Congress to make change. They made their arguments to lawmakers.

## ANTHONY'S ARREST

**In an 1872 election, Susan B. Anthony tried to vote. Others joined her. Police arrested the women. Anthony went to court. They fined her $100. She believed it was unfair. She never paid the fine.**

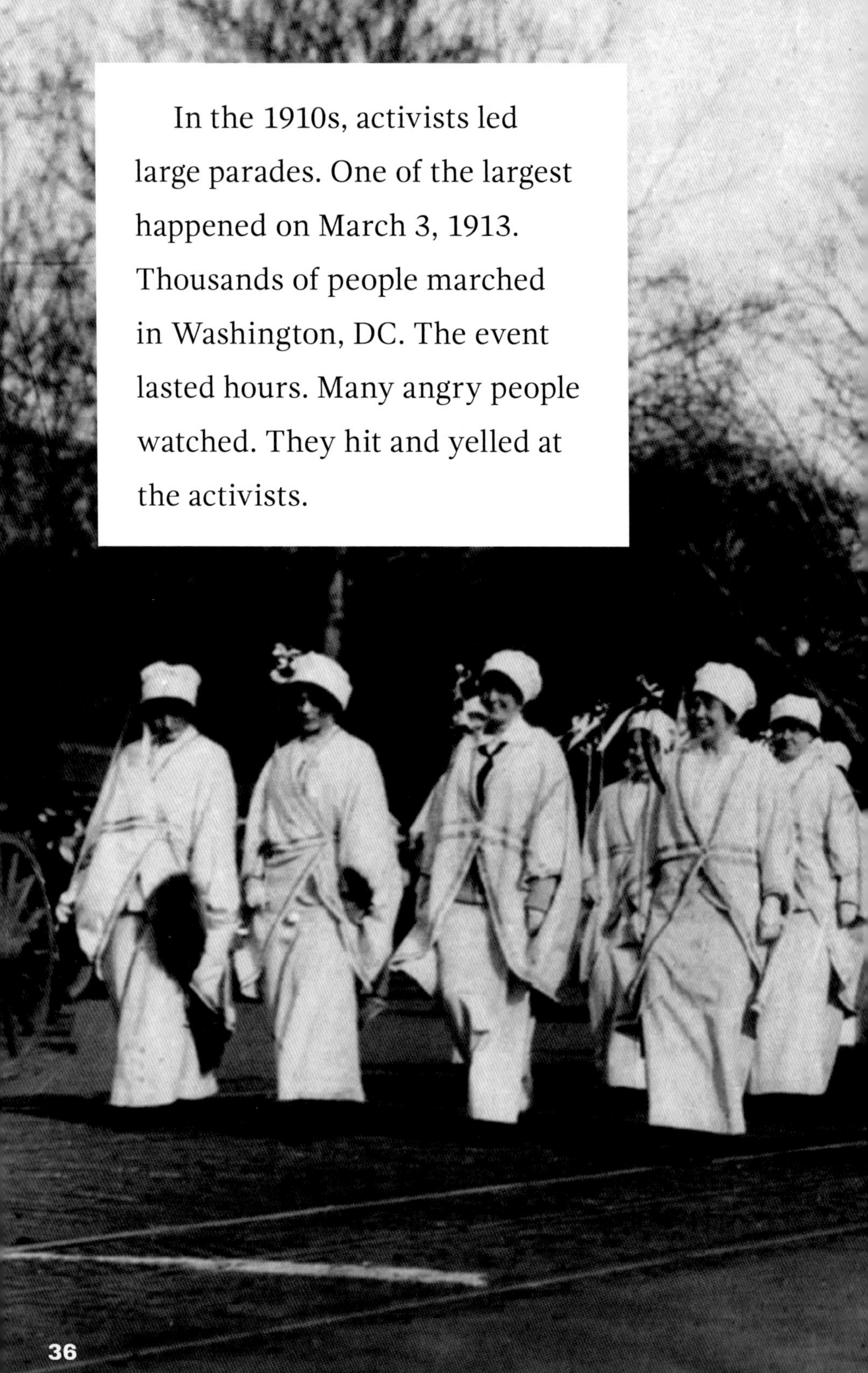

In the 1910s, activists led large parades. One of the largest happened on March 3, 1913. Thousands of people marched in Washington, DC. The event lasted hours. Many angry people watched. They hit and yelled at the activists.

## AT THE PARADE

Suffrage groups continued to separate Black women. During the 1913 parade, Black women were told to march at the back of the group. But many didn't listen. They marched next to white women anyway. Black activist Ida B. Wells-Barnett was among them.

Protesters march for women's voting rights in 1913.

The National Woman's Party was another voting rights group. In 1917, it led a picket at the White House. For three years, women stood silently outside the White House. They stood there six days a week. Police arrested many of the women. The group was inspired by British suffragists. They used similar methods.

## JAILED

Women from the picket line faced horrible jail conditions. Many women wouldn't eat. Guards force-fed and beat them. Some people felt sympathy for the women. Eventually, the court dropped all the charges.

The National Woman's Party held the first White House picket in history.

## Story Spotlight

# IDA B. WELLS-BARNETT

Ida B. Wells-Barnett was an activist. She fought against lynching. She supported civil rights and voting rights. Wells-Barnett worked hard for these goals. She organized events. She wrote in newspapers. Wells-Barnett educated people, too. Many people disagreed with her. Some wanted to hurt her. But she kept fighting. In 1913, she started a group in Chicago, Illinois. It was the Alpha Suffrage Club. It was one of the first Black women's suffrage groups.

**Wells-Barnett often called on white suffragists to also focus on lynching.**

Chapter 5

# BUILDING SUPPORT

In 1878, Congress considered an amendment for women's suffrage. But Congress didn't vote on it until 1887. The amendment failed.

Even so, some states had given women voting rights by the late 1800s. More followed in the 1900s. Many states gave women only some voting rights. For example, a few states let women vote on school-related matters.

Activists focused on states with women's suffrage to help win voting rights nationwide.

CALIFORNIA

In 1914, Congress tried again. It voted on another amendment for women's suffrage. It fell short of passing. In 1917, women gained voting rights in New York. It was one of the first eastern states to do so. By 1918, 15 states had given women voting rights.

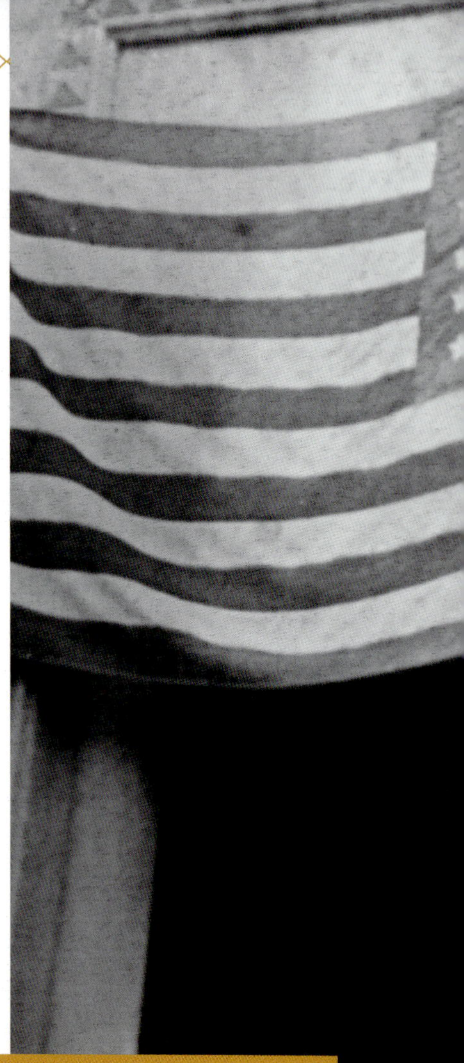

## PAVING THE WAY

In 1916, Jeannette Rankin was elected to the House of Representatives. She became the first woman in Congress. She fought for women's voting rights. She also supported rights for workers and families. Rankin showed that women could be in politics.

Throughout her life, Jeannette Rankin worked for women's rights and against war.

Activists helped change President Woodrow Wilson's stance on women's suffrage.

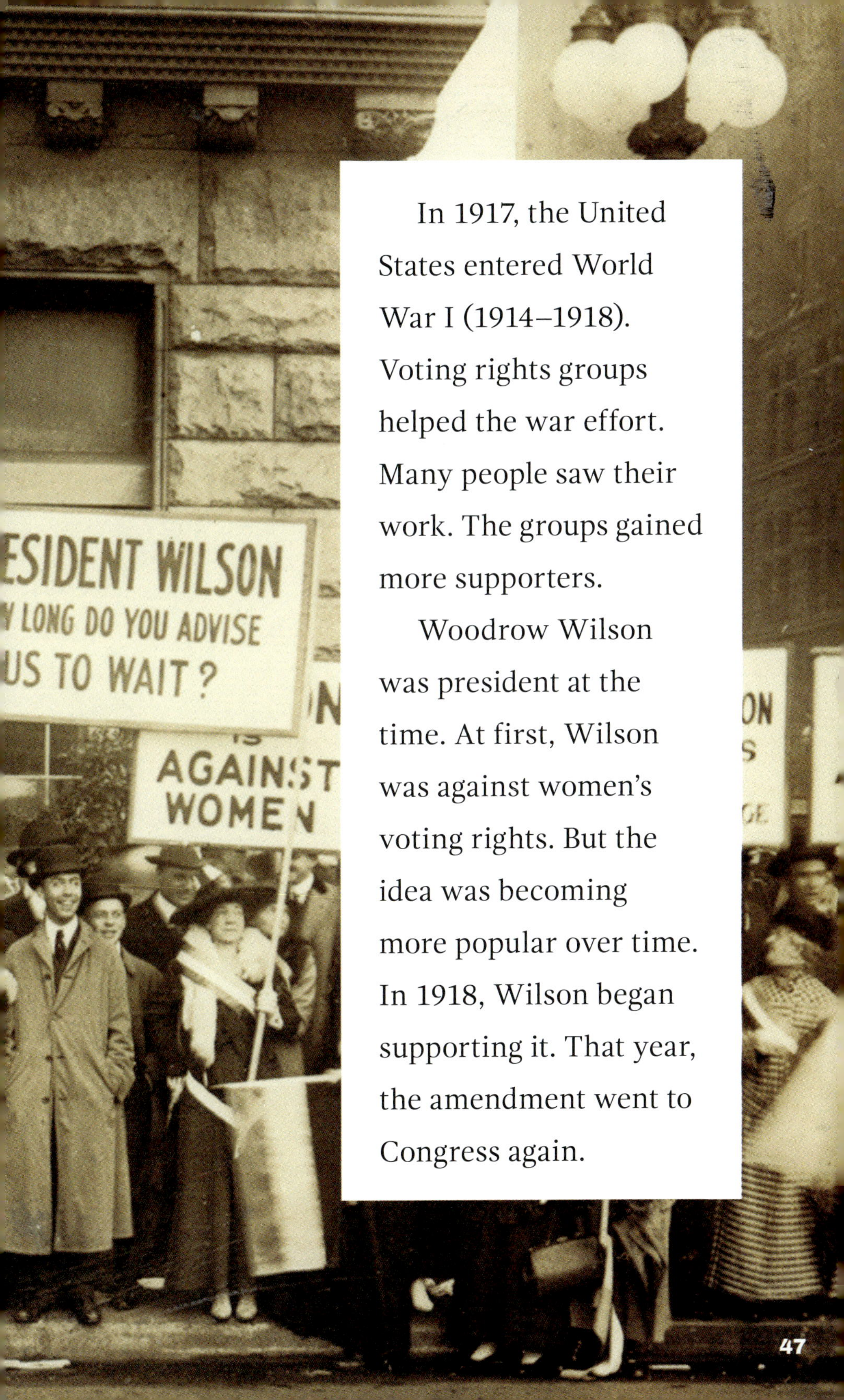


In 1917, the United States entered World War I (1914–1918). Voting rights groups helped the war effort. Many people saw their work. The groups gained more supporters.

Woodrow Wilson was president at the time. At first, Wilson was against women's voting rights. But the idea was becoming more popular over time. In 1918, Wilson began supporting it. That year, the amendment went to Congress again.

In January 1918, the House passed the amendment. But the Senate voted against it. In May 1919, the House passed it again. In June, it passed through the Senate. But the job was still not done. Next, the amendment went to the states.

## STATE RACE

For an amendment to pass, three-fourths of the states need to support it. Each state votes one by one. In 1919, 22 states voted for the amendment. By March 1920, 35 states had. But the next three states voted against. Finally, Tennessee passed it in August.

Missouri's governor signs the amendment for women's voting rights in July 1919.

Women cast their votes in the November 1920 election.

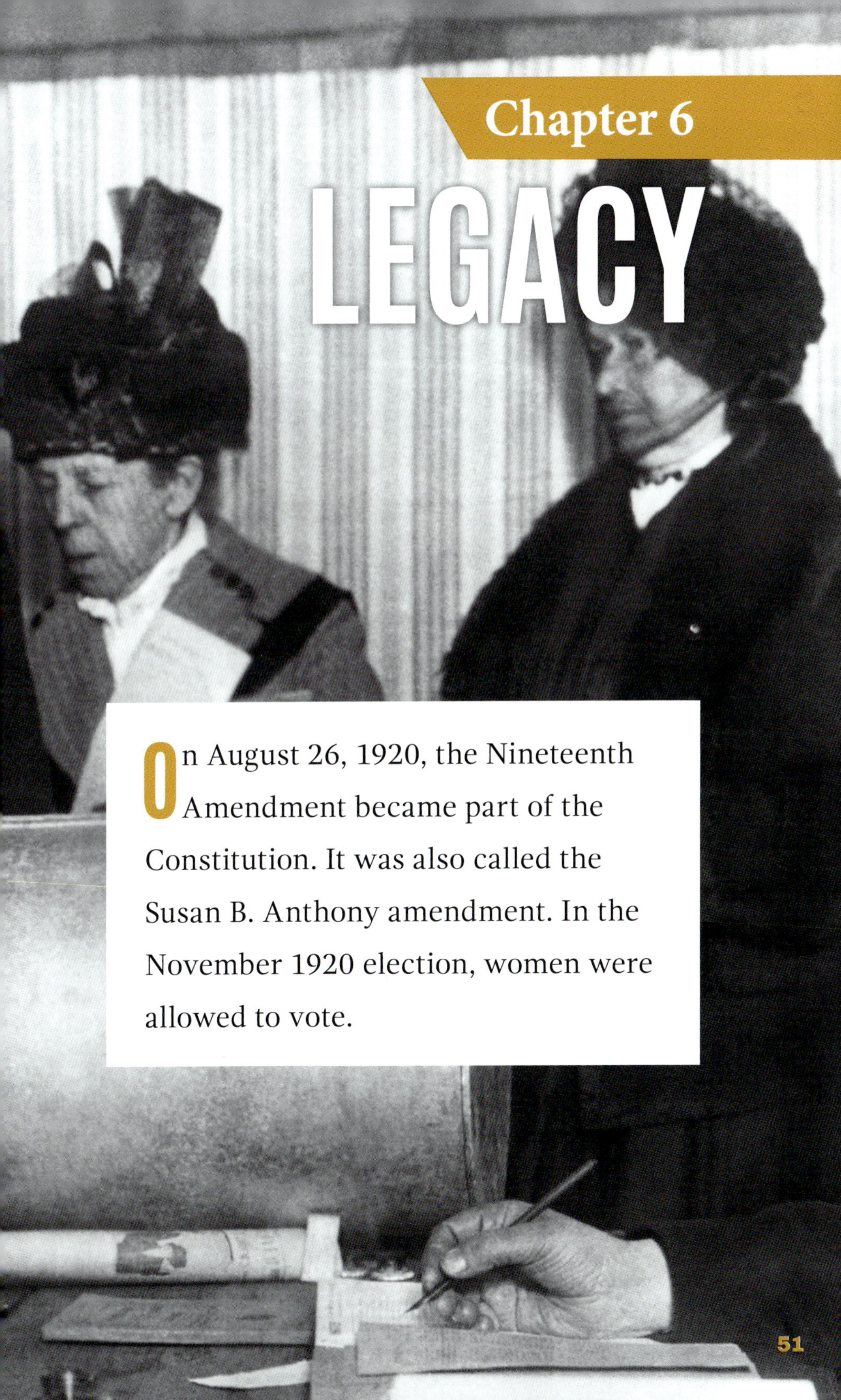

Chapter 6

# LEGACY

On August 26, 1920, the Nineteenth Amendment became part of the Constitution. It was also called the Susan B. Anthony amendment. In the November 1920 election, women were allowed to vote.

In 1920, NAWSA leaders formed the League of Women Voters. This group continues to support women in politics today.

However, many women didn't vote in 1920. Some states made it difficult. For example, the amendment passed after registration deadlines. So, many women weren't registered to vote. Some states said those women couldn't vote. Other women grew tired of politics after World War I. So, they didn't vote.

Many women of color were also blocked from voting. They faced discrimination. People tried hurting them. Some white activists ignored Black women. But women of color kept fighting. The Civil Rights Act passed in 1964. The Voting Rights Act passed in 1965. These laws let many more women vote.

## INDIGENOUS AND IMMIGRANT WOMEN

In 1920, Indigenous people were not considered US citizens. So, they couldn't vote. In 1924, the Snyder Act gave them citizenship. Many immigrants also couldn't vote. It took years and more laws for that to fully change.

Activist Fannie Lou Hamer helped win voting rights for Black people in the 1960s.

In 2021, Kamala Harris became the first woman to serve as vice president of the United States.

For many years, women voted at lower rates than men. That finally changed in the 1980s. In the 1990s, women began winning more and more seats in Congress. Today, women still hold fewer seats than men at all government levels. Women had less than 30 percent of seats in Congress in 2024. But women continue to fight for equality.

## SECOND WAVE

The fight for voting rights was the first wave of feminism. The second wave came in the 1960s and 1970s. Women fought for equal pay. They also fought against mistreatment based on gender. This wave worked to include women of color. It brought more women into politics.

# TIMELINE

**JULY 19–20, 1848**
Activists meet at the Seneca Falls Convention to discuss women's rights.

**MAY 12, 1869**
Suffragists disagree about the Fifteenth Amendment. They later split into two groups.

**JANUARY 10, 1878**
The first women's suffrage amendment is introduced to Congress. It does not pass.

**FEBRUARY 18, 1890**
The two women's suffrage groups join to create the National American Woman Suffrage Association.

**MARCH 3, 1913**
Thousands of women parade through the streets of Washington, DC, calling for suffrage.

**JUNE 4, 1919**
The Nineteenth Amendment passes through Congress.

**AUGUST 18, 1920**
Tennessee becomes the 36th state to pass the Nineteenth Amendment.

**AUGUST 26, 1920**
The Nineteenth Amendment officially becomes part of the US Constitution.

# COMPREHENSION QUESTIONS

*Write your answers on a separate piece of paper.*

1. Write a paragraph that explains the main ideas of Chapter 3.

2. Do you think all suffragists should have supported the Fifteenth Amendment? Why or why not?

3. When did Congress first consider a women's suffrage amendment?

   A. 1878
   B. 1914
   C. 1920

4. Why would Susan B. Anthony try to vote when it was against the law?

   A. She didn't care about voting laws.
   B. She wanted to show that voting laws were fair.
   C. She wanted to show that voting laws were unfair.

5. What does **convention** mean in this book?

*In July 1848, the Seneca Falls **Convention** took place in New York. Elizabeth Cady Stanton and Lucretia Mott set up this meeting.*

A. a law

B. a vote

C. a gathering

6. What does **risk** mean in this book?

*Adding women to the amendment was a **risk**. It could have killed the amendment.*

A. a choice to keep things the same

B. a choice that is very safe

C. a choice likely to go wrong

*Answer key on page 64.*

# GLOSSARY

**amendment**
A change or addition to a legal document.

**Constitution**
The document that lays out the basic beliefs and laws of the United States.

**discrimination**
Unfair treatment of others based on who they are or how they look.

**feminism**
The belief in equal rights for women and men.

**immigrants**
People who move to a new country.

**Indigenous**
Related to the original people who lived in an area.

**lynching**
When a person is killed by a mob without a court deciding if the person was guilty.

**petitions**
Formal requests that many people sign and send to a leader.

**racist**
Having to do with hatred or mistreatment of people because of their skin color or ethnicity.

**suffrage**
The right to vote.

**traditional**
Using beliefs or ways of doing things that began long ago.

# TO LEARN MORE

## BOOKS

Felix, Rebecca. *#WomensMarch: Insisting on Equality*. Minneapolis: Abdo Publishing, 2020.

Loh-Hagan, Virginia. *Women's Rights*. Ann Arbor, MI: Cherry Lake Publishing, 2022.

Orr, Tamra. *Susan B. Anthony's Women's Right to Suffrage Speech*. Ann Arbor, MI: Cherry Lake Publishing, 2021.

## ONLINE RESOURCES

Visit **www.apexeditions.com** to find links and resources related to this title.

# ABOUT THE AUTHOR

Abby Doty is a writer, editor, and booklover from Minnesota.

# INDEX



## ANSWER KEY:

1. Answers will vary; 2. Answers will vary; 3. A; 4. C; 5. C; 6. C